Finance 101 for Kids

Money Lessons Children Cannot Afford to Miss

Finance 101 for Kids

Money Lessons Children Cannot Afford to Miss

Walter Andal

Mill City Press | Minneapolis, MN

Finance 101 for Kids: Money Lessons Children Cannot Afford to Miss

Mill City Press, Inc.
322 First Avenue N, 5th floor
Minneapolis, MN 55401
612.455.2293
www.millcitypublishing.com

First printed in the United States of America
10 9 8 7 6 5 4 3 2 1
ISBN-13: 978-1-63413-943-4
LCCN: 2016902418

Book Design by Jaime Willems

Printed in the United States of America

Acknowledgments

I wish to thank the following people for their contributions in creating this book:

My editor, Lisa Rojany, for her professional advice, guidance, and time spent in polishing the manuscript.

My illustrator, Richard Peter David, for his skills, patience, and hard work.

To Michelle Brown, Ali McManamon, and the Mill City Press team for consistently providing world-class customer service.

To Candace Roy, Grace Mamolo, and Jenniffer Brescini, for their insights, feedback, and support.

And most especially, to my amazing wife, Anne, for always standing by my side. She is my rock and my inspiration.

I dedicate this book to our four wonderful children: Gabriel, Angelo, Jacob, and TJ, who are the best children any dad could hope for.

Contents

Foreword to Parents   ix

Introduction: Welcome to the Class!   **xiii**

Chapter 1: What Is Finance?   **1**

Chapter 2: Money: How Did It All Start?   **7**

Chapter 3: How to Earn Money   **13**
   A. Working for Someone   13
   B. Working for Yourself Providing Goods or Services   16

Chapter 4: The Power of Money   **19**
   A. Making Your Money Work for You!   19
   B. Money Works for Others, Too!   23

Chapter 5: Introduction to Credit   **27**
   A. What Is Credit?   28
   B. The Great Things About Credit   29
   C. The Not So Great Things About Credit   32

Chapter 6: Dealing with Credit   **35**
   A. Different Types of Credit   35
     1. Credit Cards   35
     2. Student Loans   38
     3. Automobile Loans   40
   B. Getting Credit   41
     1. Character   42
     2. Capacity   44

Chapter 7: Save Your Money! **47**
  A. Why Bother to Save?   47
     1. To Prepare for the Big Purchases   47
     2. To Prepare for Emergencies and Unexpected Expenses   49
  B. Budget: A Great Tool to Help You Save   50
  C. Banking Tools to Help You Save   52
     1. Savings Account   53
     2. Checking Account   53
     3. Debit Cards and ATMs   56
     4. Certificate of Deposit   57

Chapter 8: Money and Our Economy **61**
  A. Demand and Supply   62
  B. Inflation   66
  C. Unemployment   68

Chapter 9: The Stock Market **71**
  A. What Is a Stock Market?   74
  B. Making Money in the Stock Market   76
     1. Share in the Profit   76
     2. Rise in the Price of Stocks   76
  C. The Down Side of Stock Market Investing   78

Chapter 10: Money Around the World **81**
  A. What Are Currencies?   81
  B. What Is Foreign Exchange?   83
  C. Other Uses of Foreign Exchange   85

Afterword: Sharing Makes Sense! **87**

References **93**

Foreword to Parents

While strolling in a shopping mall, my then nine-year-old son Angelo sees a huge Nintendo 3DS XL display at a video game store. He politely asks if I would buy him this new handheld game console. I tell him that I do not have enough money to make a purchase at that moment. Then he naively replies, "But Dad, you don't need money. Just use your credit card!"

Similar to Angelo, many children of elementary school age still think that using credit cards to shop does not require spending money. After making more inquiries, I found out that many middle school children have a limited understanding of savings, credit, investments, and finance even though these kids might be performing well academically.

You know the importance of managing your personal finance. You use your financial knowledge when making budgets, applying for loans, and investing. A bad financial decision can greatly affect your life. Understanding basic finance is therefore a necessity in today's world. Yet even though you know how important finance is, children rarely get opportunities to really learn finance in school. Schools introduce the *concept* of finance during the children's economics and math classes in high school, but the majority of kids never take a class in the actual mechanics of finance, such as understanding how credit cards work and learning the effects of too much debt and late payments. Finance is reinforced only to a few students who will opt to take finance courses during college.

As a parent, I strongly believe that I need to teach finance to my children as early as possible. Just like how playing sports promotes perseverance and teamwork, how practicing martial arts fosters self-control and discipline, and how music and arts encourage creativity and self-expression, a timely education and training in finance promotes good financial habits. In this world of e-commerce and increasing consumerism, children need to have a solid understanding of finance before they get overwhelmed by huge student loans, owing massive amounts on credit card debts, and not controlling their spending.

My mother taught me and my siblings the value of money and savings at a very young age. She motivated us to save by opening an individual savings account for each of us and made us deposit the money we saved from our weekly allowance and the money we received as presents. She also taught us to be conscientious with spending. I applaud my mother and the other parents who have done a marvelous job of teaching their kids early about money and finance. For those who have not started to do so, there is no reason to feel bad. It is never too late to start teaching finance to kids. For those parents who are uncertain about their own financial knowledge, take a few minutes to re-learn basic finance—and pass on the knowledge to your children.

This book is written to introduce finance in an informative and entertaining manner. Although the target audience of this book is middle school students between the ages of 8 to 12, any person of any age with limited or no prior knowledge of finance will benefit from *Finance 101 for Kids*. This book is not intended to transform kids into know-it-all investors or business tycoons (although that would be a marvelous consequence), rather, the main goal is to present basic yet important information for children to develop financial responsibility and help them make smart financial decisions early in their lives.

Introduction:

Welcome to the Class!

Hi! My name is Mr. Buckingham. My students call me Mr. Buck. I teach math and history a lot of the time, but what I really love most is teaching money matters to kids like you. This class will introduce you to the world of finance. You will have a great time learning more about money. And don't worry! This class will be entertaining. In fact, five of your classmates sitting in the front row volunteered to help me make this class more exciting. You can thank Ben, George, Andrew, Olivia, and Chloe in advance for their help.

Ready to start? Let the fun and learning begin!

Chapter 1:

What Is Finance?

Money—anything acceptable that can be used to exchange for goods and services

Goods—real items that can be seen and touched

I love to teach about **money** because money is valuable and useful. It has become an important part of our everyday lives. Money enables us to buy **goods** like video games, clothes, books, and smartphones. Many people enjoy shopping. With money, you can buy many of the things you want.

Services—work that is provided by another person

Spend—using your money for payments or purchases

Save—setting aside your money for future use

Money also allows you to obtain **services**. Your parents pay a mechanic to repair the car, a gardener to mow the lawn, a plumber to fix a water leak, and a doctor to check on you when you get sick. You may not know this, but the electricity, the cable TV, and the Internet services you use at home are available to you because of money.

When you receive money, you have a choice to either **spend** it or **save** all or some of it for the future. There is nothing wrong with spending money, especially for buying goods and services you truly need; however, saving money is also very important because it helps you prepare for the expensive items you need to purchase in the future such as a college education, a car, and a house. More importantly, saving money allows you to better handle unexpected expenses and emergencies that can happen in the future.

Investing—putting money somewhere it can grow

Savings—money set aside for future use

Charities—organizations that provide help for those in need

What is exciting about money is that it can grow when it is put in the right place. This is called **investing**. Any person, young or old, can invest **savings** and earn more money. The sooner you start to invest your money, the bigger your savings can grow over time.

Here is the best part. Besides spending, saving, and investing, did you know that money empowers a person to help a community? With money, you can support **charities** and make a difference in someone's life. It surely feels great when you are able to help someone and contribute to a worthy cause. You'll learn more about this later.

Because there are so many wonderful things you can do with money, nearly everyone dreams of having lots of money. But money is not easy to come by. Have you heard of the expression "Money does not grow on trees"? This means money is not something you can easily get like picking an apple from a tree. People need to work in order to earn money.

Are your parents working? Most parents work for a living. Grownups normally work eight hours a day, five days a week. Some work even longer than that. Making money takes a lot of time, energy, and skill. But the rewards of having a job can be far more than just making money. Helping to create something, giving back to the community, handling an interesting service—all of these and more are good things that come from having a job.

> **Investments**—something that you purchase with the hope that it will provide income or will be more valuable in the future

But there are also some not-so-good realities you need to face when dealing with money. When someone buys more than what he or she makes, that person could end up with no money in the future. Sometimes, people can also lose money when they put their savings into the wrong **investments**. When you don't properly manage and protect your money, you can lose it. You get stressed out when you lose that hard earned money—especially when you cannot buy the things you need.

Finance—the way money is obtained, managed, and used

Learning how to make money and how to take care of your earnings is a responsibility that you cannot take for granted. This is where the knowledge of **finance** becomes very useful. Finance, in a nutshell, is the process of managing money. Learning finance will help you make good choices when it is time for you to decide on how you will earn and make money. More importantly, understanding how money works allows you to make smarter decisions as you spend, save, and invest your money.

This is a great day to learn finance! There is more to come in the following chapters.

Chapter 2:

Money: How Did It All Start?

Thousands of years ago before money was developed, people were self-sufficient. They took care of themselves and their children in their small villages. Life was simple. They survived primarily by means of hunting. When they ran out of their food supply, they moved from one place to another. During that time, there was no need for money.

> **Specialize**—choosing one thing to be really good at
>
> **Productivity**—being able to make goods or provide services
>
> **Bartering**—the exchange of goods and services without the use of money

As time went by, many people developed special skills. Some learned to raise cattle, pigs, and sheep. A few became good at planting crops and grains, while some developed skills in fishing, carpentry, mining, and crafting. People learned to **specialize**, which means to choose one thing to be really good at. With specialization, **productivity** increased, meaning that people produced more than what they needed.

Specialization encouraged people to trade with each other for goods they were unable to produce or for tasks they could not perform. For example, a farmer would need the help of a carpenter to build a house, and a carpenter would need a farmer to get food. Trading started, but no paper bills or coins were used. People then were **bartering**.

Bartering is the exchange of goods and services without the use of money. It is similar to trading baseball cards, swapping video games, or switching homemade lunches with your buddies. Before money was developed, a farmer could trade a cow for two pigs, or a carpenter could offer to build a barn in exchange for food and tools.

Bartering works as long as one person finds another person willing to trade and accept the goods or services being exchanged. But it does not always work. If the cow farmer believes that the value of his cow is at least equal to two pigs, what will happen if he cannot find a pig farmer who has two pigs to trade? What if the pig farmer only has one small pig? Will the cow farmer trade his cow for bread or a tool instead? Most likely, the cow farmer will not trade his cow if he cannot find something that is at least of same value. If he cannot find one, no exchange will take place. Therefore, bartering does not always work as it can be difficult to find a match for the items being traded.

Instrument of exchange—*anything that can be used to make a trade*

Transaction—*buying or selling of goods and services*

Note—*a piece of paper that promises to pay the holder*

As trading expanded, people learned to trade more goods including precious metals such as gold and silver. Because gold was rare, beautiful, and could be molded into bars, gold was accepted as a common form of payment. The value of the gold was determined by its weight. Trading thrived because gold was widely accepted as an **instrument of exchange**.

The use of gold for trading has its own drawbacks. When the **transactions** became bigger, the traders were burdened with carrying heavy loads. Can you imagine how much gold a trader needed to bring if he wanted to buy a farm or a big boat? The solution: Traders found it easier to leave their gold with another person like a goldsmith or a banker for safekeeping. The goldsmiths and banks issued **notes** written on paper stating how much gold had been left with them. The person holding the note had the option to go to the bank and exchange the note with gold, or he could continue to use the note for other transactions. Guess what happened next? Because the notes were valued by actual gold, the notes circulated in the marketplace. Traders accepted those notes as payments for goods and services. As a result, notes or paper bills (one dollar bills, five dollar bills, twenty dollar bills, etc.) became regular instruments of exchange. Coins started out as gold and silver, but soon changed into copper and other mixed metals.

Interestingly, the money you use today is no longer backed by gold, and the paper itself used to print money has very little value or worth. So the question you might have is "Why does my money remain valuable?"

Government—the group of people who leads a nation or a community

Guarantee—a promise that a condition will be fulfilled

Stability—being strong and less likely to change or fail

To keep your money valuable, the **government** has to **guarantee** its value. A guarantee is a promise that a certain condition will be fulfilled. The value of the money you use today is guaranteed by the government, and you trust the government's guarantee. This system of the government providing their guarantee and the people trusting the government helps maintain the **stability** and value of our money.

Chapter 3:

How to Earn Money

Income—money received from someone else

Salary—the payment to the worker for the service done

Business—an activity that brings income through selling goods or services

Employee—a person working for another person or organization for pay

Employer—the person or organization providing the jobs

Corporation—an organization formed by a group of people acting together; a corporation can be a company or a business, too

People need **income** to obtain money. There are many forms of income. It can be received in the form of a **salary**. It can be earned as a profit from having a **business.** It can be from an investment. Or it can be a gift from friends and family. Let's look at some different sources of income.

A. Working for Someone

To earn money, you need to work for it. Most grownups earn money by having jobs. A person who works for someone is called an **employee**, while the one who provides the job is called the

employer. The employer may be an individual person, a **corporation**, or the government. The employee receives a salary as payment for the work that was done for the employer.

What does your parent do for a living? Have you thought of the type of work you want to do when you grow up? Some jobs pay more, but may require more schooling and training. The chart below shows some jobs you may want to consider in the future. The chart also displays the average yearly salary in the United States, and the amount of schooling and training needed to get into these occupations.

Salary Estimates in the United States (2015)

Job	Average Yearly Salary	Years in School/Training
Airline Pilot	$101,852	4 years in college, training in a flight academy, plus a lot of flight experience
Carpenter	$41,354	3–4 years of training
Computer Programmer	$58,436	2–4 years in college
Dentist	$123,922	4 years in college plus 4 years in dental school
Doctor/ Physician	$138,248	4 years in college plus 4 years in medical school then at least 3 years of residency/training
Elementary School Teacher	$41,561	4 years in college
Electrical Engineer	$70,675	4-5 years in college
Financial Analyst	$56,469	4 years in college
Firefighter	$43,915	2–4 years in college plus training in a fire academy
Lawyer	$77,251	4 years in college plus 3 years in law school
Police Officer	$48,336	2–4 years in college plus training in a police academy
Registered Nurse	$57,672	2–4 years in college

When choosing a career, you need to remember this: You should look not only at the salary or the prestige associated with the work. It is also very important that you enjoy the kind of work you do.

B. Working for Yourself Providing Goods or Services

Self-employed—a person who earns a living by working for himself or herself

Profit—the money made from running a business as a result of having more revenues than expenses

Have you met someone who owns a store, a shop, a business, or a restaurant? These people earn money by working for themselves instead of working for an employer. They are referred to as **self-employed** or business owners. They make money by having a **profit** from the business they own.

Revenue—the money made from selling goods or services

Expense—the money spent for running the business

The profit can be figured out by adding up all the **revenues** and subtracting all the **expenses**. The revenues are the income made by the business from selling goods or services. Expenses are the money spent for running the business. Expenses may include the money used to pay for materials, office supplies, equipment, rent, and employee salaries. The basic formula to figure out profit is:

Profit = Revenues – Expenses

A business makes a profit when the total revenue is greater than the total expenses. The goal of every self-employed person, just like most business organizations, is to consistently make a good profit. A profitable business means the owners are making money. The profit can be used to grow and expand the business.

Loss—the opposite of profit; the result of having more expenses than revenues

When the expenses are greater than the revenue, the business is experiencing a **loss**. During a loss, more money goes out than the money that comes in. No self-employed person or business organization wants to have a loss. If the business continues to experience a loss, the owners may be forced to shut down the business.

Chapter 4:

The Power of Money

A. Making Your Money Work for You!

Interest—the payment for the use of money

Deposit—putting money in a bank

Your money can grow over time because of the **interest** it can earn when **deposited** in a bank. Interest is the money the bank pays you so they can use your money for its own investments. In other words, banks pay you interest because when you deposit your money, you are allowing them to use your money for their business.

Principal—the original amount of money invested

Interest rate—the percentage rate paid for the use of money

Term—a period of time for an investment or a loan

To figure out the amount of interest, you need to know three numbers:

- The original amount of money, also known as the **principal.**
- The annual (yearly) **interest rate.** The interest rate is the rate paid for the use of money, and is shown as a percent.
- The length of time the money will be left in the bank. Also known as the **term.**

These three numbers are multiplied together to get the amount of interest earned.

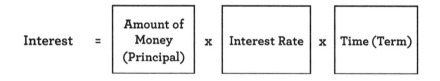

As an example, let's say George deposited $1,000 of his savings to SaveMore Bank. This bank is paying three percent interest per year. How much interest will he receive in three years?

Using the formula we just learned:

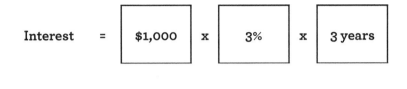

$$\text{Interest} \quad = \quad \boxed{\$1,000} \quad \text{x} \quad \boxed{3\%} \quad \text{x} \quad \boxed{3 \text{ years}}$$

Interest   = $90

George's $1,000 will earn $90 in three years or $30 per year. The $90 earned in three years may not seem very exciting. But how much money will George earn in three years if he keeps his $1,000 savings under his bed? Zero! That $90 of interest earned in three years is much better than nothing at all!

Now think of how much interest George will earn if he increases the amount of money he deposits in the bank. Add two zeroes to his initial deposit, making his total deposit $100,000. His interest for three years will be $9,000 (we just add two zeroes to the interest earned). This is equal to $3,000 per year! Amazing, right?

B. Money Works for Others, Too!

Depositor—a person or an organization that puts money in the bank

Borrower—a person or an organization that uses someone else's money for a period of time

Lender—a person or an organization that lends money in order to make a profit

Just like most businesses, the banks operate to make profits. Because banks have money from the **depositors**, or the people who put money in the bank, the banks can lend that money to its own clients. The banks make money by lending the money at a *higher* interest rate than what the bank pays you in interest.

To show how banks make profits, assume that one of SaveMore Bank's clients, Chloe, borrowed $1,000 to buy a new oven for her bakeshop. In this scenario, Chloe became a **borrower**, while SaveMore Bank became a **lender**. SaveMore Bank used the money George deposited earlier, and lent it to Chloe. If SaveMore Bank charged seven percent interest to Chloe, how much will she pay if she used the borrowed money for three years? Using the same formula you learned earlier, you figure out the interest like this:

Interest   = $1,000   x   7%   x   3 years

Interest   = $210

At the end of the third year, Chloe will pay $210 to SaveMore Bank. This $210 is revenue for the bank. So how much profit does the bank make from this simple transaction? Go back and use the basic formula on how profit is made:

Profit = Revenues – Expenses

Profit = $210 interest from Chloe – $90 interest paid to George

Profit = $120

This is a simple illustration of how a bank makes money through the use of your deposits. Banks have many clients who put their money in the bank and many clients who borrow money from the bank. For example, Bank of America listed in its website that in 2014, it had more than $1.1 trillion in deposits, and made a whopping $4.8 billion profit!

The interest rates that banks offer to its depositors and borrowers are not fixed. Rates can change over time because of different factors. For example, in the year 2000, some banks were paying interest rates of up to five percent to the people who put their money at the bank. The downside of this was that people who needed to borrow money had to pay higher interest rates. This was necessary so the banks could make money.

In comparison, the interest rate paid by banks to its depositors went down to less than one percent in 2014. People who depended on income from their bank deposits were hurt by the low interest rates. Nevertheless, the low interest rates were good news for people who had to borrow money. This means that the interest they paid to the bank for big purchases like houses and cars was lower compared to what they paid 15 years before.

Chapter 5:

Introduction to Credit

Credit—an arrangement that allows a borrower to get something valuable and pay the lender in the future

Credit Card—a small plastic card that allows a borrower to buy goods and services on credit

Loan—the money borrowed from someone with a promise that the money will be paid back in the future

Mortgage—a type of loan used to buy a house

A. What Is Credit?

Have you seen your mom buy groceries without using money? She swipes a plastic card in front of the register, signs a piece of paper, then takes off with the grocery items. Did she just get the groceries for free? Not at all! She bought the groceries on something called **credit**.

Credit is an agreement between a borrower (in the above example, Mom) and a lender (the bank) in which the borrower gets something valuable and promises to pay for it in the future. Credit allows the borrower to get money, goods, or services, and immediately enjoy its benefits while delaying the payments for it. All money, goods and services gotten through credit arrangements have to be paid fully at some time in the future. Usually the total amount of payment made is more than the original price you paid because when a borrower uses credit, the lender charges you interest for using the borrowed money.

There are many ways lenders provide credit services to their clients. The credit may be in the form of **credit cards**, auto **loans**, student loans, and home loans; home loans are also known as **mortgages**. You may not notice it, but utility companies (gas, electricity, cable, water) also provide credit services. In your home, you are using credit every time you turn on the lights, flush the toilets, watch shows on cable TV, surf the Internet, and use your cellphone. The utility companies give credit to your parents, and they allow your family to use their services immediately. Your parents will pay for the amount they use at a later time.

B. The Great Things About Credit.

Cash—money in the form of bills and coins

Debt—the amount of money a person or business owes

Statement—a report that shows how you used credit for the past month

There are many good things about using credit. When people don't have enough **cash**, they can still get the things they need and want by using credit, then pay off their **debts** (the money they owe) when money becomes available. Credit also allows people to borrow money against their expected future income. This is very helpful when purchasing expensive stuff such as a house, a car, or a college education. With credit, families are able to buy a house. People can buy cars to get to work. Credit allows students to go to colleges and universities as they go after their dreams.

Credit makes buying more convenient and safer. With credit cards, you do not have to bring a huge amount of cash with you, especially when traveling. Credit allows you to buy goods and services online or through your smart phone. The **statements** you receive from the lenders also provide you with a good record of what you have spent, what you have paid for, and what you owe.

Businesses and governments use credit to grow and expand. With credit, businesses can get money to buy supplies and materials needed even though they are short on cash. They use credit for huge purchases such as buying factories, equipment, and vehicles. Businesses pay off their loans as they make profit.

Tax—the money you contribute to the government to help pay for government projects and public services

The government also uses credit to pay for big projects like new roads, bridges, walkways, and buildings. The government repays their debts with money they collect through **taxes**. A tax is the money you contribute to the government to help pay for those big government projects and public services (such as police and the armed forces, schools, libraries, hospitals, parks, and postal service).

C. The Not So Great Things About Credit

Even though credit benefits a lot of people, credit can also be harmful. Remember that everything you buy with credit has to be repaid with interest at some time in the future. That time in the future is specific, not just anytime you want to pay it back; there are deadlines. Not using credit correctly can cause a situation in which debts get too big and out of control.

Overspending—using more money than you should

Bankruptcy—a situation in which a person or business is legally de-clared as not able to pay back debts

Forgiving—cancelling all or some of the debt

Credit report—a summary of the person's credit history, usually used to evaluate a person's credit standing

Because you have to pay interest for using the money you borrowed, what you owe (your debts) could pile up faster than you can repay them. **Overspending** can put borrowers in a position where they can hardly keep up with the payments. When they don't pay what they owe on time, it can result in a loss of valuable properties such as the house and the car. So if you use your credit card and you don't pay the money back on time and in full, then you can get in big financial trouble. Failing to pay loans can destroy the borrower's good reputation. There are many times when spending too much and managing credit poorly causes a breakdown in family relationships. In some countries, failure to pay back loans is punishable by jail time. In many countries, a person with unmanageable debt might be forced to declare **bankruptcy**.

Bankruptcy is when a person or a business is no longer able to repay the debt he or she owes. Bankruptcy offers an individual or a business a chance to start fresh by **forgiving** the debts that can't be repaid. In the United States, bankruptcy can only be granted by a judge in a state or federal court; you have to go to court to get approval to declare bankruptcy.

Although bankruptcy wipes away most debts, declaring a bankruptcy has long lasting bad effects. Since bankruptcy will be reported in your **credit report**, it could keep you from getting new loans, or it may increase the interest rates that you will need to pay to get a loan. Filing a bankruptcy involves a complicated and expensive process which will take time away from school, work, and family. Also, bankruptcy can interfere with getting a new or different job. Employers can investigate credit reports before making job offers. A bankruptcy on your credit report may push the employers to offer the job opportunities to other possible employees who have shown greater responsibility with managing their personal finances.

Chapter 6:

Dealing with Credit

A. Different Types of Credit

Let's look at the different types of credit that students like you will probably encounter in the near future.

1. Credit Cards

A credit card is a small plastic card issued by banks and other businesses to its clients. A credit card allows the cardholder (the person allowed by the bank to use the credit card, usually the person whose name is on the card) to buy goods and services on credit. The banks work with credit card associations like Visa, Master Card, and American Express to process the purchases made with credit cards. The cardholder can use the card worldwide because it is accepted in millions of places around the world.

Store Credit Card—*a credit card given by big stores; can only be used for purchases in that store*

Discount—*selling of goods or services at a lower price*

Rebate—*returning a part of the payment you made*

Big stores like Target, Sears, Home Depot, and Macys provide **store credit cards**. Store credit cards work like a regular credit card. The main difference is that most store credit cards can only be used to buy goods and services at the stores of the provider. Because of this restriction, getting a store credit card is easier than getting a regular credit card that you can use anywhere. Those stores also give **discounts, rebates**, and other rewards designed to benefit shoppers who come back again and again.

The banks charge interest for the use of the credit card when the purchases made are not paid in full every month. So every month, you will get a statement in the mail or online from the credit card company telling you how much you owe and when you have to pay it by. If you don't pay the full amount during the grace period, which may be 15 to 30 days from the date you got the statement, the credit card issuer or bank will charge you a very high interest rate, ranging from 10 percent to 24 percent per year. That means that almost a quarter of the amount you spent could be added on in interest! So a $100 purchase could become $124 that you owe if you don't pay it back in full. If the cardholder does not make the minimum payment on time, the interest rate can even go much higher. On top of the interest, the banks can also charge a separate late fee if you are late in paying back, making what you bought a lot more expensive than the original price because of all the added fees.

Cash advance—borrowing money in the form of cash from a credit card company

Bank teller—a bank employee who helps customers with their banking needs

Check—a piece of paper that tells the bank to pay the stated amount to another person or business

Credit cardholders can also take out cash using their credit cards. This is called a **cash advance**. A cash advance is like asking the credit card company to give you money that you can spend on anything you want. You can get cash through an Automated Teller Machines (ATMs), a **bank teller** inside the bank, or by asking the credit card company to send you a **check**. Cardholders can get cash up to a certain limit. But it is not a good idea to take cash advances using a credit card because the fees and interests associated with this are very high. Cash advances should only be used during emergencies and must be paid off immediately as soon as money becomes available.

THIS IS WHAT BILLIONAIRE INVESTOR MARK CUBAN SAID WHEN ASKED WHAT HE WISHED HE KNEW ABOUT MONEY IN HIS TWENTIES.

Lessons from the Pro

"That credit cards are the worst investment that you can make. That the money I save on interest by not having debt is better than any return I could possibly get by investing that money in the stock market."

2. Student Loans

Going to college is one of the best decisions you can make for yourself. Studies show that people with college degrees earn much more during their lifetime than those without college degrees. But a college education can be expensive, especially if you go to one of the very famous private colleges and universities.

Student loan—money borrowed to pay for educational expenses

Repayment—paying back the money owed

To pay for a college education, students usually apply for **student loans**. This loan can be used to pay for school tuition, books, computers, and living expenses. The good news with student loans is that **repayment** (paying it back) does not start until the student is done with school. This allows the student to focus on studying and not to worry about the payments while he or she is still in school. The bad news is that this loan cannot be cancelled or erased even if you did not like the education you received, you did not get a job related to your degree, you are having a hard time financially, or you declared bankruptcy. Therefore, any student who wishes to apply for a student loan must seriously think about the total amount he or she will borrow as well as how he or she plans to repay the loan over the years. You certainly do not want to be drowning in a flood of debt when you are done with college.

39

3. Automobile Loans

Down payment—*the first bigger payment required when buying more expensive goods and services on credit*

Balance—*the amount of money still owed*

Installment—*multiple equal payments made by the borrower until the loan is paid in full*

Car title—*a paper that identifies the legal owner of the vehicle*

Grownups can use automobile loans to purchase new or used cars. Auto loans are provided by banks, car manufacturers (the ones who make the cars), and sometimes, by the car dealers (the ones who sell the car). This is a one-time loan which means the lender will release the money one time to complete the sale of the car. Oftentimes, the car buyer will be required to pay a portion of the sales price called **down payment** up front and right away. The **balance** (the rest) will be repaid by the car buyer in equal monthly payments called **installments**. Auto loans can have a term of up to seven years, meaning you can take up to seven years to pay off the loan and the interest. Although the borrower gets to take the car, the **car title** remains with the lender until the borrower has fully paid the loan. The car title is a legal form that identifies and certifies the legal owner of the vehicle. Once the borrower has paid off the auto loan, the title will be transferred to the borrower's name.

B. Getting Credit

Not everyone who applies for a credit card or a loan can be approved. The banks give credit to qualified people applying who can and will pay back the loan. But how can a bank know that the person applying for a loan is a good borrower and will pay back what they promise to?

Banks have several ways of figuring out if they are going to give credit or not. To get a credit card or loan, you have to fill out an application form that asks you a lot of question about your financial life. Although banks look at several things when figuring out the credit-worthiness of the borrower, most banks care most about the borrower's character and capacity. Let's look at each of these.

1. Character

> **Character**—*the reputation and the traits of the borrower in hand-ling money and debts*
>
> **Credit history**—*a record of how responsible the borrower is with paying his or her debts on time*
>
> **Credit score**—*the numerical grade or rating you received based on the information in the credit report.*

Character refers to the reputation of the borrower. Character shows the willingness of the borrower to repay the loan. Banks figure out the borrower's character by reviewing the borrower's **credit history, credit score**, educational background, and work experience.

When a person applies for credit, the lender or bank will get the applicant's credit report. The credit report tells about the person's credit history including his or her track record of paying back debts on time and the amount of debt that is still owed or still has not been paid off in full.

The credit report also provides the person's credit score. The credit score rates how the borrower has managed past loans and the amount of loans they still have to pay off. A borrower with more than one or two late payments will have a lower score. Having too many loans to pay (such as too many credit cards with money owed on them) can also pull down a credit score. The credit score plays a big part in the bank's decision on whether to loan the money or give the credit card as well as the interest rate that will be offered to the borrower. People with high credit scores will most likely get an approval on their loan application. They will also receive good interest rates. On the other hand, the banks may decline the loan applications of a borrower with a very low credit score. If you have a low credit score and the credit card company or bank still decides to loan you the money or give you a credit card, then you will probably get charged a higher interest rate.

Taking care of your credit reputation is a very important responsibility. If you do not pay your debts on time, this will haunt you in the future when you apply for loans. Having a bad credit reputation costs a lot because lenders will charge you higher interest rates. The higher the interest rates you pay for your loans, the more money goes out of your pocket.

Even though Ben and Andrew bought the same car worth $10,000 at the same time with the same terms (5 years), Andrew pays more every month because of his low credit score.

2. Capacity

> **Capacity**—the ability to pay back the loan
>
> **Co-signer**—a person with a good credit standing who signs the loan document with the main borrower, also becoming responsible to pay back the loan if the main borrower stops making payments

Capacity refers to the borrower's ability to repay the loan. When a person applies for a loan, the banks will look at the borrower's income, how stable his or her job is, how many other loans the borrower owes money on, and how much he or she has paid back. Having a stable job (one that has lasted or should last) and good income shows that the borrower can make regular payments when the loan payments are due.

If the borrower's credit or employment does not look strong enough, the bank may ask for another person with a good credit history and good income to co-sign the loan. A **co-signer** is someone who will sign the loan documents together with the main borrower. The co-signer will become responsible for the loan if the main borrower stops making payments. Co-signing a loan usually happens when a student is applying for a student loan. Since the student has no credit history or stable sources of income, the lender may ask the parents to co-sign the loan application. If the student fails to make the regular monthly payments after college is over, the lender will try to collect the money from the parents or whoever co-signed the loan.

When getting a loan and having a co-signer, remember that you need to be extra responsible in paying off what you owe when you owe it. Any missed payment will not only damage your reputation, but will also harm the reputation of the people who generously co-signed for you.

Chapter 7:

Save Your Money!

A. Why Bother to Save?

At the start of this class, you heard me say that saving money is important. With how easy it is to get credit cards and the convenience of buying almost everything online, shopping just got a lot easier and more tempting than before. There are many reasons why you need to save, but here are two reasons to help you realize the importance of savings.

1. To Prepare for the Big Purchases

At a young age, it is okay to wish for the latest smartphone, a new tablet, a bike, an electric scooter, or an iWatch as a holiday or birthday present. You should always be thankful for all the gifts you get, even for those that are not included in your wish list. If you did not receive an item from your wish list that you really want, why not help your parents buy it for you by contributing some money toward the cost of the item? You can do so by saving some money from your allowance or from the cash gifts you receive during your birthday or holidays. Your parents will surely appreciate this wonderful gesture. The more money you contribute toward the cost, the higher the chances are that your parents can buy it for you.

When you grow up, there are really expensive things you may want to buy. You might need a car to drive you to work or a house for your own family. One day, you might decide to go after a higher university degree or extra training to boost your career, or maybe you go back to school so you can switch careers. You might want to have a memorable and colorful wedding, or you might want to travel and explore faraway destinations with your loved ones. You can do all of these things especially when you have savings to back you up.

Risk—the chance or the possibility of losing money

When buying expensive items like a car and a house, most people apply for a loan. Having money set aside for a down payment can help you get a loan with reasonable interest rates. Banks like it when you give bigger down payments because it lowers their **risk** of you failing to pay back the loan. Likewise, when you provide a big down payment, it lowers the amount of money you need to borrow, and makes your monthly installments more affordable.

With a $500
Down Payment

I will pay
$184 a month
for the next
5 years

With a $2,500
Down Payment

I will only pay
$145 a month
for the next
5 years

Notice the difference when George pays a bigger down payment for the purchase of a $10,000 car at 6% interest rate with a term of 5 years.

2. To Prepare for Emergencies and Unexpected Expenses

As the saying goes, life is full of surprises. You surely like happy surprises, but sometimes unpleasant surprises can also come when you least expect them. Your car could break down and might require huge repairs. A pet dog might get sick and need to see a veterinarian. A water pipe could burst causing a flood inside the house. You might have to fly to attend a funeral of a loved one. You might unexpectedly lose your job.

Emergencies and unexpected expenses can put a lot of pressure on your wallet. But if you have money set aside for events like these, you will be in a better position to handle the challenges brought about by these unwanted surprises. That's why saving money is so important.

B. Budget: A Great Tool to Help You Save

Budget—*a plan of how much you will spend and save for a period of time*

Live within your means—*spending no more than what you have or what you can afford*

There are so many things you can buy at the local store or online. With all the choices you have, it can be difficult to decide how you will spend your money and how you can still save a portion of it for the future. For that reason, having a **budget** will be helpful in managing your money.

A budget is a plan of how much you will spend and how much you will save for a period of time. Making a budget is important because a budget allows you to figure out the amount of money you can spend, where you will spend it, and the amount of money you can set aside for savings. Following a budget keeps you out of debt because it enables you to **live within your means**. In other words, a good budget helps avoid overspending.

When making a budget, you need to list all the sources of your income on one side and add them up. Your income includes the allowance you get from your parents, the money you receive from having a job, and the money you receive as presents. On the other side, you need to list all your expenses for that period of time and add them up. Subtract the total expenses from the total income. Should you choose to donate money, you will need to subtract this amount from your income, too. If the difference is a positive number, this means you are saving. Otherwise, if the final number is negative, this means you are overspending.

As an example, let's look at how Ben uses a budget to manage his money.

Ben's Budget for the Week

INCOME
Weekly allowance	$25	
Gift from Grandma	5	
Total Income		$30

EXPENSES
Food	$15	
Drinks	5	
Book purchase	3	
Pencil	1	
Total Expenses		$24
Donation to Church		$1
Amount Saved		**$5**

You can see from Ben's budget that he is not overspending. He figures out where he will use his money. And in the process, he saves five dollars! Ben is doing a wonderful job making a good budget and managing his money.

C. Banking Tools to Help You Save

Insured—*guaranteed against losing the money*

Deposit account—*an arrangement with a bank that allows a person or an organization to put in and take out money*

Withdraw—*to take out money from the bank*

The bank is probably the best place to safely store your money. Banks have fire-proof steel vaults that can only be opened by certain individuals under very tight security. In the United States, the money deposited in banks is **insured** by a government agency called FDIC, which stands for Federal Deposit Insurance Corporation. This means that even if the bank ran out of money, got robbed, or burned down, you can still get back your money up to $250,000 per bank through the FDIC.

Banks offer several ways to keep your money safe and to make it more convenient for you to handle your finances. Let's look at some of them.

1. Savings Account

A savings account is a **deposit account** used by individuals and businesses mostly to save and protect their money. The money deposited in a savings account earns a small amount of interest. The money can also be **withdrawn** any time the bank is open.

Almost anyone can apply for a savings account. Some parents open savings accounts for their children when they are very young to encourage them to save. A savings account helps you to be smart about your money because the money saved in a bank is harder to get compared with money stored in a savings jar. And remember, your money grows while in a savings account because of the interest you earn for letting the bank hold and use your money to lend to other people or to other businesses.

2. Checking Account

Have you seen your parents write a check to pay water and electricity bills? Did you receive a check as a birthday present? What did you do with the check?

Like a savings account, you also deposit money into a checking account. Unfortunately, most checking accounts do not pay interest. What makes the checking account special is that it allows you to use that piece of paper called a check to buy goods, pay for services, or give money to another person or an organization.

Payee—the person or business a check is made out to

Bounced check—a check that is not accepted because there's not enough money in the account

When your mom writes a check, she is in a way ordering her bank to pay a specific amount to the **payee**, who is the person or the business to whom the check is made out to. Your mom needs to have enough money in her checking account to make the payment successful. Your mom cannot write an amount greater than what she has in her checking account, or else the check will **bounce.** If your mom's check bounces, the bank will charge her a fee. A fee will also be charged to the payee by the bank where the bad check was deposited.

People use checks because it is easier and safer to carry a checkbook than a bunch of cash in your pocket. Cash can be easily stolen whereas a check is only good if it is signed by the owner of the checking account. When making payments by mail, checks are safer because only the payee can deposit the check in a bank or exchange the check for cash. Checks also give you a permanent record of a payment, that way you can better keep track of payments you make with checks.

3. Debit Cards and ATMs

> **Debit card**—a card that lets you take money directly out of your
> checking account to make a purchase

Debit cards and ATM cards are two good ways to get money out of your savings or checking accounts. Debit cards look like credit cards, but they are not credit cards. You can use a debit card to purchase goods in a store just like when you are using a credit card. But the debit card is electronically tied into your checking account. Every time you use the debit card, the money is automatically taken from the checking account right away. A debit card will only work as long as you have money in your checking account. Unlike credit cards, a debit card does not allow you to borrow money from the bank.

When you were younger, you might have thought that ATMs were money machines that magically gave away money. Unfortunately, there is no such thing as a magic money machine. ATMs are electronically linked to your savings and checking accounts. Withdrawing money from an ATM is similar to going to a bank and taking out money from a bank employee called a bank teller who stands at a window and helps you do what you need to do inside a bank. With an ATM, the transactions are processed through a machine. You can deposit or withdraw money anytime or anywhere you can find an ATM. Careful, some ATMs charge an extra fee to use them.

4. Certificate of Deposit

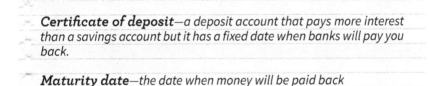

Certificate of deposit—*a deposit account that pays more interest than a savings account but it has a fixed date when banks will pay you back.*

Maturity date—*the date when money will be paid back*

A **certificate of deposit**, also known as CD, is similar to a savings account, but the money in a CD earns more interest than money in a savings account. A certificate of deposit has a **maturity date**, which is the time when the bank pays back your money plus the interest you have earned. You can choose the maturity date you want when you open a CD account. It can be anywhere from three months all the way to five years. The interest rates you earn usually get bigger the longer you leave the money in a CD.

Banks provide higher interest rates on CDs in exchange for a guarantee that the depositors will keep the money in the bank until the maturity date. If you withdraw the money before the maturity date, the bank will charge you with an early withdrawal fee. This is why CDs are sometimes called "time deposits."

A smart way to manage your savings is to balance the money you deposit into your savings, checking, and CD accounts. If you do not expect to make a big purchase in the next few months or years, it makes a lot of sense to put a big chunk of your savings into CDs so your money can earn more interest income for you. It is also a good idea to leave some money in your savings or checking accounts to be used for emergencies and unexpected expenses.

.

Chapter 8:

Money and Our Economy

You heard a newscaster mention the word *economy* in a report, or your parents talking about the economy over dinner. What is so important about the economy? Does it have anything to do with your money?

> **Economy**—*the way a nation uses its limited resources to produce goods and services*
>
> **Resources**—*the supplies used to produce goods and services which may include materials, land, money, and people.*

The **economy** is the way a nation or a country uses its limited **resources** to produce goods and services. A healthy economy means the country is making good decisions and using its resources—such as land, materials, workers, and money—to create more products and services. You benefit when the economy is growing because more jobs are available and businesses are making money. The opposite is true when the economy is weak. People may be losing jobs and businesses may be closing down. Many people and businesses are hurt financially when the economy is weak.

Let's take a closer look at some factors that can affect the economy and you.

A. Demand and Supply

IT WAS LESS THAN $3 LAST WEEK. WHY DOES THE PRICE OF GAS CHANGE?

Demand—the desire and willingness to buy goods or services

Supply—the availability of goods or services

Have you ever wondered why the prices of gasoline, food, and other goods keep changing? Although business owners can set the prices of the goods and services they offer, the two main factors affecting price are the **demand** and the **supply**.

Shortage—*a situation when there is not enough to satisfy a need; it happens when the demand is greater than the supply*

Surplus—*a situation when there are leftovers after meeting all the needs; it happens when the supply is greater than the demand*

Demand is your wanting and willing to buy the goods or services, and supply is how available or easy to get the goods or services are. Generally, when the demand is greater than the supply, a **shortage** occurs, which forces prices to go up. Prices go up when the demand is higher because people are willing to pay more for an item that they badly need or want especially when there is a shortage of that item. Similarly, when there are more available items than what we want (supply is greater than demand), a **surplus** occurs, which forces prices to go down. Prices can go down when there is a surplus because the sellers will likely lower the price to encourage buyers to make a purchase. When supply and demand are equal, the price tends to be stable.

Here are some examples of how changes in demand and supply can affect the price:

• During championship games for major sports like football, basketball, and baseball, more fans want to see the championship games live inside the stadium. The supply of game tickets to enter the stadium is fixed since the stadium can only hold a certain number of people. The price of the game tickets goes up.

• With the release of iPhone 6, the demand for older versions (iPhone 4 and iPhone 5) goes down as more people choose to buy the latest version. The price of the older versions of iPhone goes down.

• A fire in a gas refinery causes a shutdown. The supply of the gasoline falls because there is not enough gasoline produced to meet the demand. Gas price goes up.

• Grapes are plentiful during the year because of good growing weather. There are more grapes than what people would normally buy. The price of grapes falls.

Having a good knowledge of demand and supply can help you make good choices when spending your money. If you know that the demand for an item is still very high, you might consider waiting for the demand to go down, and buy the item at a later time when the price is lower. Say you have a smartphone and find out that a newer version is coming up. Is it really worth buying the latest smartphone at its highest price when the demand is very high? Can you wait a little bit to upgrade your phone only when it is really necessary to make that switch? Or when you watch a movie, do you go with the big crowd that watches the movie at night when the movie tickets are more expensive than daytime showings? An understanding of the concept of demand and supply can actually help you save some money and make you a smart shopper!

B. Inflation

Did you know how much a gallon of milk cost in 1975? It was $1.57. In 1995, the price was $2.41. By September 2015, the cost of a gallon of milk was $3.39. Why does the price of milk keep going up over the years?

Inflation—the general increase in prices of goods and services

Prices of goods and services go up because of **inflation**. There are several reasons inflation can happen, but the main reason is the increase in the demand without a similar increase in the supply. For example, when people have more money due to an increase in salary or more access to credit, they tend to spend more. Remember, when the demand is greater than the supply, prices will go up.

Let's look at the estimated price of other items in 1975, 1995 and (September) 2015:

Items	1975	1995	2015
Gallon of regular gasoline	$0.57	$1.15	$2.38
A dozen eggs	$0.77	$1.16	$2.97
First-class stamp	$0.13	$0.32	$0.49
Average sale price of new homes	$42,600	$158,700	$296,900

When inflation occurs, our money can buy less. For instance, when the price of movie tickets increases by 10 percent, the movie ticket that cost $10 a year ago will now cost $11. Therefore, more money is needed to buy the same amount of goods and services. Imagine if there are five of you in the family, your family will pay an extra $5 this year to go to a movie.

Because of inflation, it is not smart to keep all your savings in a piggy bank. Use your piggy bank only to save money until you can put it in your savings account. When you put your money in a place where it is not growing, chances are the money you have will have less value when you use it in the future.

Inflation can also be difficult for people who are living on a fixed income like older people who are retired; this is because they usually have less money than they did when they were working, and their buying power gets smaller during times of high inflation. Their $20 today would only buy a portion of the groceries they used to buy way back in 1995. Although the rate of inflation changes every year and it is normal to have an inflation of one to two percent every year, there were times in the 1970s and 1980s when inflation reached twelve percent. When prices are rising by twelve percent every year, the price of goods and services will double in six years. This means your money will be worth half in six years when the prices are rising by that much.

Effects Of Inflation

1975   1995

2015

C. Unemployment

Unemployment—the number of people who are looking for work but cannot find a job

The **unemployment** number is an important way of telling if the economy of our country is healthy. Every week, the government releases the unemployment number, which is the number of people who are able, willing, and looking for work but cannot find a job. When unemployment is high, only a few job opportunities are available for people looking for work. People with no jobs will have tougher times getting the goods and services they need, resulting in fewer sales and profits to businesses, which in turn results in more jobs being cut. This cycle continues until the economy turns around and gets better.

When making financial plans, you should always take into account the possibility of losing your job. People should have money set aside for emergency situations. People who are in a lot of debt are also pushed to the edge when an unexpected job loss happens. This reminds you of the importance of living within your means, and not overusing credit cards even though you think that you can afford to pay back the money using your future income.

Chapter 9:
The Stock Market

Let's start this topic by telling you the story of Cupcake Avenue, the bakeshop that Chloe started. Chloe is the only owner of Cupcake Avenue, which means she owns 100 percent of the business. Her customers like the cupcakes, and she sells all of the cupcakes she bakes every day. After just one year in business, Cupcake Avenue becomes a popular bakeshop.

Because of the growing demand for her cupcakes, she realizes she needs to buy two more ovens to keep up with the orders. She thinks of applying for another loan at SaveMore Bank, but because she does not want to pay interest, she invites her two friends, Olivia and Ben, to invest in her business and become part owners. They all agree that Olivia and Ben will each invest $1,000 in the business to help Chloe buy two ovens. In return for their investments, Olivia and Ben will get 25 percent ownership each. If Chloe were to sell the business, she still owns half or 50 percent of Cupcake Avenue.

Share—*a unit of ownership in a business*

When Chloe sells half of Cupcake Avenue to Ben and Olivia, she is dividing the ownership of the company into four equal parts or **shares**. Chloe gets two shares which represent 50 percent (2 shares x 25 percent) of the company while Ben and Olivia receive one share each. One share represents 25 percent ownership.

At the end of the year, Cupcake Avenue makes a profit of $300. Chloe, Ben, and Olivia decide to use $100 to buy more supplies, and distribute the remaining $200 of profit among the owners. The $200 is divided into four (since there are four shares in the business), so each share gets $50. Since Chloe owns 50 percent or two shares in the company, she gets $100. Ben and Olivia each receive $50 because they own one share each.

A few months later, George hears about Cupcake Avenue's success. He gets interested in joining the company as a part owner, too. He makes an offer to buy one share of the company for $1,000. But none of the owners accept his offer. Later, George increases his offer to $1,200. Olivia accepts the offer and sells her one share to George.

Cupcake Avenue remains profitable. Chloe, Ben, and George are very happy about the success of the business.

A. What Is a Stock Market?

Stock market—the place where the stocks or shares of publicly listed companies are bought and sold

Stock—part of a company that can be traded

Investor—someone who provides money with the expectation of a gain or profit

Shareholder—a person or an organization that owns one or more shares in a company

Stockbroker—the person or online company that is authorized to buy and sell stocks for investors

Besides depositing your money in a bank to grow, another option where you can invest your money is the **stock market**. The stock market, sometimes called the stock exchange, is a place where you can buy and sell company stocks. A **stock** or a share is a part of a company that can be traded. A stock represents a share of ownership in the company. When you buy a stock, you become a part owner of that company.

The concept of how a stock market works is similar to the story of Cupcake Avenue. When a company needs money to grow, the owner can sell a portion of the company to **investors**, the people who buy the stocks or shares. Then these investors become part owners of the company. Investors in stocks are also called **shareholders**. Ben and Olivia become shareholders of Cupcake Avenue when they bought one share each at $1,000.

Stocks are traded all over the world. The New York Stock Exchange (NYSE) is the largest of these stock exchanges where the stocks of about 2,800 companies are traded. An individual investor like you can purchase stocks through a **stockbroker**. Trades can be done by calling a stockbroker or by placing an order online through a stockbroker's website.

B. Making Money in the Stock Market

Stock market investors can make money in two different ways:

1. Share in the Profit

> **Dividend**—a part of the profit that is paid to the shareholders

Shareholders are the owners of the company. If the business they own is profitable, they can share in the profit. Using the case of Cupcake Avenue, this company made a profit of $300 during the second year of its operation. The $200 profit that Chloe distributes to the shareholders is called the **dividend**.

2. Rise in the Price of Stocks

If a company is profitable and has a promising future, more investors will likely buy its stock. A bigger demand for the stock will push its price higher (remember the relationship between demand and supply?). The reason someone invests in the stock market is to sell theirs stocks above the price they paid for them. As in the case of Cupcake Avenue, Olivia made a profit when she sold her stock for $1,200, which is $200 more than her purchase price of $1,000.

Usually, a big chunk of the money made in the stock market is through the rise in the stock prices. Let's look at some of the companies you might know, and see how their stock prices changed from November 2012 to November 2015.

Name of Company	* Nov. 1, 2012	* Nov. 2, 2015	Percent Change
Hershey	$73	$88	21%
Mattel	$38	$25	-34%
McDonald's	$87	$112	29%
Microsoft	$27	$53	96%
Nike	$49	$131	167%
Walt Disney	$50	$ 115	130%

Stock Prices are rounded off to the nearest dollar

Note the changes in the prices after three years. Imagine if you invested $1,000 in McDonald's stocks in 2012, your money would be worth about $1,287 after three years. How much is your investment worth in 2015 if you decided to invest $1,000 in Nike stocks in 2012? Your money would be worth about $2,673! Isn't that wonderful?

C. The Down Side of Stock Market Investing

The stock market has been a great channel for investors to make good money. But investing in the stock market involves high risk. Look back at the chart and check the stock price of Mattel, the maker of Barbie dolls and Hot Wheels toys. Although this company and their products are popular, their stock price dropped from $38 in 2012 to $25 by November 2015. This means if you invested $1,000 in Mattel in 2012, your money would only be worth $657 after three years.

In contrast to what happens to the price of the stock when the business is profitable and promising, the stock price will go down when the company is not making good profits, or when the company is losing customers to its competitors. Investors do not like companies that are performing poorly. When there are many investors selling a stock (supply is greater than the demand), this will create a downward pressure on the price of that stock, making its price go down.

Because investing in stocks can be risky and there is a possibility of losing money, you need to do a lot of research before investing in any stock. You should know what the company does, their financial history, and how successful their products and services are. Also, you need to know who they compete with, how aggressively they compete in the market, and how promising and useful their products and services are. People will likely invest more in a business that is growing and profitable.

HERE ARE SOME WORDS OF WISDOM FROM BILLIONAIRE INVESTOR WARREN BUFFET WHEN INVESTING IN THE STOCK MARKET.

Lessons from the Pro

"We don't have to be smarter than the rest. We have to be more disciplined than the rest."

Chapter 10:

Money Around the World

A. What Are Currencies?

Currency—the type of money used in a country or area

Political stability—having a strong and successful government

Currency is the type of money used in a country or area. There are more than 190 countries in the world, and every country is either using its own currency or is sharing a common currency with another country.

The currency in the United States is called the *dollar*. In China, it is called the *yuan*. In the Philippines, it is called the *peso*. In Europe, several countries have agreed to use one currency called the *euro*. The countries using the euro include Austria, Belgium, Cyprus, Estonia, Finland, France, Germany, Greece, Ireland, Italy, Latvia, Lithuania, Luxembourg, Malta, the Netherlands, Portugal, Slovakia, Slovenia, and Spain. Other European counties like Denmark, Poland, Sweden, and the United Kingdom are accepting the euro, but they still use their own currencies, too.

There are more than 160 currencies around the world. But the value of one currency is different from another. What a currency is worth depends on several factors including the demand and supply of the currency, the strength of the economy, and the **political stability** of the country or region.

B. What Is Foreign Exchange?

Foreign exchange—the conversion of one currency into another currency

Because the values of the currencies are different, you may need to convert your money to a foreign currency when you travel abroad. This is needed especially if you plan to buy foreign goods or services. The conversion of one currency into another is called **foreign exchange**. You can exchange currencies in a bank, at money changing stores, or at foreign exchange kiosks inside the airports. These money changing stores post the exchange rates on big display boards.

These are the steps you can follow to find out the equivalent amount of money in the new currency you need:

Step 1: Know the amount of money you want to exchange.

Step 2: Find out the exchange rate between the two currencies.

Step 3: Multiply the amount of your money by the exchange rate to get the value of your money in the new currency.

George lives in the United States, and he is traveling to the Philippines for a business trip. He wants to buy $200 worth of items that he can bring back to the United States. Let's help George convert his U.S. dollars into Philippine pesos.

Step 1: Know the amount of money you want to exchange:	**$200**
Step 2: Find out the exchange rate between the two currencies:	**47.17**
Step 3: Multiply the amount of your money by the exchange rate to get the value of your money in the new currency:	$200 x 47.17 = **₱9,434**

C. Other Uses of Foreign Exchange

International trade—the exchange of goods and services between countries

Import—goods and services purchased from another country

Export—goods and services sold to another country

Foreign exchange is widely used in personal and business travel, but it is actually used more in **international trade**. International trade is the exchange of goods and services between countries. Because of innovations in transportation and communication, almost every country is now able to trade more goods and services with other countries. Goods and services bought from another country are called **imports**, while products and services sold to another country are called **exports**.

In 2014, the United States bought $119 billion worth of oil from Canada, $130 billion worth of electronic equipment from China, and $46 billion worth of vehicles from Japan. When you buy goods from these countries, you need to convert your dollars into their currencies.

In a similar way, other countries import goods from the United States. In 2014, Canada imported American vehicles amounting to $51 billion. China bought aircrafts worth $14 billion dollars, while Japan imported $4 billion worth of cereals. For those countries that want to buy American goods and services, they may need to exchange their currencies into US dollars.

Afterword:

Sharing Makes Sense!

At the start of this class, you identified the different things you can do with your money. You can spend it on goods and services. You can save it for the future. You can invest it and make more money for you. Or you can give it back to the community.

You learned that money is not easy to come by. Most of you need to work to earn money. It may seem unfair to give back some of the money you earned to benefit other people. But let's explore why it is worthy to give back.

Sharing makes sense because the money you give back to the community can make a difference in someone's life. Sadly, there are many people on this world who are not as lucky as you are. But you can do something to make them feel good and help them live a better life. One way to do this is by donating to charities. A charity is an organization that helps people in need. When you donate money to charity, your money will be pooled together with the other donations, and it will be used to help the charities accomplish their missions. Even a small amount can make an impact—especially if this is used to help people who live in extreme poverty. A $1.00 donation, for instance, can provide a person in poor country with access to safe drinking water for a year. A $3.00 donation can buy books to help children from poor families expand their knowledge.

In June 2015, American billionaire Warren Buffet donated $2.8 billion dollars to charities. Mr. Buffet's total donation to charities has reached $23 billion. Imagine how many books, food, and gallons of clean drinking water this amount can buy. You might say that Mr. Buffet is super rich, and he can afford to donate billions of dollars. Indeed, Mr. Buffet is a multibillionaire. But you don't need to be a billionaire or a millionaire to give back to the community. You can always start with a very small amount and go from there. You can also give non-cash donations while you are still not earning money. Some charities accept toys, books, canned goods, school supplies, old equipment, and used clothing. Those charities distribute the donated items to people in need, or they can sell the goods to raise money. Remember that your donation, no matter how big or small, can become a powerful force when pooled together with other donations.

Donating money to charities is voluntary. There are no laws or rules that require people to give money. But even without this obligation, people continue to share their wealth for various reasons. Some people feel good in knowing that they have contributed to a good cause. Some people want to actively participate in fighting poverty, promoting better health, offering scholarships, and funding medical research. Some donate money because of religious beliefs. Others donate money to get tax breaks because donating money can lower the taxes they need to pay. Whatever their motivations are, the donations help a lot in supporting the programs of the charities they choose.

Nobody is challenging you to match the money donated by Mr. Buffet. The hope here is that you will study hard, work hard, and will have high motivation to earn more when you grow up so that while you and your family are enjoying the fruits of your labor, you can also give more and help more.

Through this class, you learned how important money is, how you can make money, and how it can be used in different ways. What you do with your money is totally up to you. In the end, what matters more is not the goods and services you bought to make you look and feel good, but how you used your money to make you a better and smarter person.

REFERENCES

"10 Reasons Why You Should Save Money (Even When Borrowing Is Cheap and Easy)." *Mymoneycoach.com.* Accessed September 22, 2015. http://www.mymoneycoach.ca/saving-money/why-save-money.

"1975 Economy/Prices." *1970sFlashback.com.* Accessed July 28, 2015. http://www.1970sflashback.com/1975/Economy.asp.

"1995 Economy/Prices." *1990sflashback.* Accessed August 2, 2015. http://www.1990sflashback.com/1995/Economy.asp.

Asmundson, Irena, and Ceyda Oner. "What Is Money?" *Finance & Development*, Vol. 49, No. 3, September 2012. Accessed August 2, 2015. http://www.imf.org/external/pubs/ft/fandd/2012/09/basics.htm.

"Average Salaries for Americans—Median Salaries for Common Jobs." Foxbusiness.com. July 9, 2015. Accessed November 1, 2015. http://www.foxbusiness.com/personal-finance/2015/07/09/average-salaries-for-americans-median-salaries-for-common-jobs/.

Bank of America. "Annual Reports & Proxy Statements." Accessed October 30, 2015. http://investor.bankofamerica.com/phoenix.zhtml?c=71595&p=irol-reportsannual#fbid=dSyS8TA3bAB.

Biedenweg Ph. D, Karl. *Basic Economics.* Illinois: Mark Twain Media, Inc., 1999.

Biedenweg Ph. D, Karl. *Personal Finance.* North Carolina: Mark Twain Media, Inc., 1999.

Bloomberg. "Markets Cross Rates" Accessed November 15, 2015. http://www.bloomberg.com/markets/currencies/cross-rates.

Bureau of Labor Statistics. "Average Retail Food and Energy Prices, U.S. and Midwest Region." Accessed October 30, 2015. http://www.bls.gov/regions/mid-atlantic/data/AverageRetailFoodAndEnergyPrices_USandMidwest_Table.htm.

Bureau of Labor Statistics. "May 2014 National Occupational Employment and Wage Estimates United States." Accessed October 30, 2015. http://www.bls.gov/oes/current/oes_nat.htm.

"Charitable Impact Calculator." *Thelifeyoucansave.org.* Accessed October 31, 2015. http://www.thelifeyoucansave.org/Impact-Calculator.

CNN. "Markets." Accessed November 12, 2015. http://money.cnn.com/data/markets/.

"Credit Education: The Devastating Effects of Bankruptcy." *Lexingtonlaw.com.* December 9, 2010. Accessed December 7, 2014. https://www.lexingtonlaw.com/blog/bankruptcy/devastating-effects-bankruptcy.html.

Federal Deposit Insurance Corporation. "Understanding Deposit Insurance." Accessed January 27, 2015. https://www.fdic.gov/deposit/deposits/.

Furgang, Kathy. *Kids Everything Money: A Wealth of Facts, Photos, and Fun.* Washington DC: National Geographic Society, 2013.

Godfrey, Neale S. *Ultimate Kids' Money Book.* New York: Simon & Schuster, 1998.

Gower, John. "Savings 101: What is a CD (Certificate of Deposit)?" *Nerdwallet.com.* Accessed September 26, 2015. https://www.nerdwallet.com/blog/banking/savings-101-cd-certificate-deposit/.

Grabianowski, Ed. "How Currency Works." *Howstuffworks.com,* September 2, 2003. Accessed August 2, 2015. http://money.howstuffworks.com/currency.htm.

Grosvenor Jr., Charles R. "Prices in the Seventies." *Inthe70s.com.* Accessed July 22, 2015. http://www.inthe70s.com/prices.shtml.

"How Many Countries Are in the World?" *Worldatlas.com.* Accessed July 9, 2015. http://www.worldatlas.com/nations.htm.

"Job Index (United States)." *Payscale.com*. Accessed November 7, 2015. http://www.payscale.com/index/US/Job.

Kane, Libby. "What 9 Successful People Wish They'd Known About Money In Their 20s." *BusinessInsider.com*., September 8, 2014. Accessed October 24, 2014. http://www.businessinsider.com/what-ceos-wish-they-knew-about-money-2014-9?op=1#ixzz3E18B22FF.

Kapoor, Jack R., Les R. Dlabay and Robert Hughes. *Personal Finance*. New York: McGraw-Hill Irwin, 2012.

Kellaher, Karen. "Kid's Economic Glossary." *Scholastic.com*, February 2, 2008. Accessed September 26, 2015. http://www.scholastic.com/browse/article.jsp?id=3750579.

Korkki, Phyllis. "Why Do People Donate to Charity." *Bostonglobe.com*. December 22, 2013. Accessed August 7, 2015. https://www.bostonglobe.com/business/2013/12/22/nonprofits-seek-understand-why-people-give-charity/72b4B2kbKiXqNzxnQbKAtO/story.html.

M&T Bank. "Understanding the 5 C's of Credit." Accessed September 20, 2015. https://www.mtb.com/business/businessresourcecenter/Pages/FiveC.aspx.

McWhorter Sember JD, Brette. *The Everything Kids' Money Book*. Massachusetts: Adams Media, 2008.

Melicher, Ronald W., and Edgar A. Norton. *Introduction to Finance Markets, Investments, and Financial Management*. New Jersey: John Wiley & Sons, Inc., 2011.

Morrell, Alex. "Buffet Donates $2.8 Billion, Breaks Personal Giving Record." *Forbes.com*. July 15, 2014. Accessed October 31, 2015. http://www.forbes.com/sites/alexmorrell/2014/07/15/buffett-donates-2-8-billion-breaks-personal-giving-record/.

"New Residential Sales in September 2015." *Census.gov*. Accessed October 30, 2015. http://www.census.gov/construction/nrs/pdf/newressales.pdf.

"New York Stock Exchange: Company Listings." *Advfn.com*. Accessed October 31, 2015. http://www.advfn.com/nyse/newyorkstockexchange.asp.

Northwestern Mutual. "What is the Stock Market?" Accessed July 20, 2015. http://www.themint.org/kids/what-is-the-stock-market.html.

"Top US Exports to the World." *Worldsrichestcountries.com*. Accessed October 18, 2015. http://www.worldsrichestcountries.com/top_us_exports.html.

"Top US Imports from the World." *Worldrichestcountries.com*. Accessed October 18, 2015. http://www.worldsrichestcountries.com/top_us_imports.html.

United States Postal Service. "Forever Stamp Prices Unchanged." January 15, 2015. Accessed July 28, 2015. http://about.usps.com/news/national-releases/2015/pr15_004.htm.

"Value Investing Explained In 7 Quotes: Value Investing, Done Well, Can Make You Wealthy." *The Motley Fool*. Accessed October 31, 2015. http://www.fool.com/investing/val-

ue/2014/07/29/value-investing-explained-in-7-quotes.
aspx.

"What Is the Most Important 'C' in the Five Cs of Credit?" *Investopedia.com*. Accessed September 20, 2015. http://www.
investopedia.com/ask/answers/040115/what-most-important-c-five-cs-credit.asp.

"What Is the Difference Between the Five Cs of Credit and Credit Rating?" *Investopedia.com*. Accessed September 20, 2015.
http://www.investopedia.com/ask/answers/033015/
what-difference-between-five-cs-credit-and-credit-rating.
asp.

CPSIA information can be obtained
at www.ICGtesting.com
Printed in the USA
LVHW082106141118
597161LV00001B/1/P